the making of a best-seller

secrets to self-publishing

and marketing your book

the making of a best-seller

secrets to self-publishing

and marketing your book

by **Sally Fairfax**

For the struggling artist

Contents

Introduction

I'm not gonna sit here and sugarcoat anything, writing is a pain in the ass. There, I said it. So before you go on, just know that it is completely and utterly the biggest pain-in-the-ass job just like any other job — like a plumber, garbage guy, mail lady, *anything* for that matter — so you should probably know that piece of info before diving into a business like this. If you're doing it for easy cash, fame, or any level of actual fortune, just quit now while you're ahead. Writing is not for you.

I'm like that tough-love mother. I'm not going to coddle you, I'm not going to motivate you, I'm not even going to *claim* you are good at writing. I'm here to help, and lifting your spirits, I'm afraid, will not bring you success in this writing business. And as Rick from *Rick & Morty* the TV show would say, "Gotta rip that bandaid off quick, now, Summer." It actually is beneficial to view the writing business as a chore, an actual competitive *job*, a job that is just as bad as McDonald's minimum wage or something . . . because it is. The reason why viewing the writing business in this light will help you is because the entire process of writing and actually publishing your work is like throwing a cast out into the ocean and wanting to catch a damn *Whale!*: think

James Patterson or Stephen King and their success, that's the Whale I'm referring to.

So in the meantime, the only thing you should worry about, as far as casting into the ocean goes, is not expecting to catch anything. If you get a little fish or a medium-sized bass, the goal is to go out, try, and just have fun. I know that's cliché and is probably turning you off from the title of this book which is based on "success in the writing industry," and that's kind of the point. I want every single one of those kinds of buyers of this book to get a thousand miles away from here, because they are a waste of my time, and frankly, a waste of yours if you want to end up doing business with or along side them. Literally never trust anyone who tells you they will give you success, including *my* lame-ass!

This all said, again, I'm your soul-crushing, tough-love-advocating mother and I want what's best for you in every way possible. But I want you to know if you are going into this wanting success, you are sadly mistaken, my ignorant child. This crap is work. And a lot of it is a hustle more than actual success. I'm telling you right now, you will have a million shitty days before you run into that one day of success. So you have to ask yourself: *Is my 15-minutes worth it? Is it worth it to literally uproot everything in my life for a pipe dream?* Because, frankly, any and all writers who claim they want success are just holders of pipe dreams. You will know a good writer from a bad writer based on how they discuss their career. If they go into it not expecting anything, doing it because it gives them some level of solace and fulfillment, and *success being secondary* and more *appreciated* than expected, that, my child, are those good writers.

I don't care if you are writing a book with the main character being an old talking sock inside a trailer home — though am I crazy or wouldn't that be a damn cool *book?* — I want you to know any and all ideas for books can be good ideas and can be done great depending on writer talent, but if you expect the world to grant you recognition or favors or to call you "great" or "good at writing" or give you any satisfaction in that sense of the word, get out of this business as quickly as possible because this is never, ever, ever, EVER going to pan out for you. Period. . . .

So without further ado, lets get this show on the road so you can publish your next garbage best-seller. *Did she just suggest that ALL best-selling books are trash?!* Yes, my ignorant child. I most-certainly did. *smiles*

Part 1: The Writer's Goal

1.1 Being a reader before being a writer.

Before ever deciding to write, you have to know exactly what you like as far as your tastes go in literature. You must firstly think of yourself as a reader before you ever even think to write, because, let me be the first to tell you, you're going to be spending a hell of a lot more time reading than you are writing. In that sense, you have to fully give up the idea of yourself getting paid, and always be a customer first. Be more excited in *other* people's work than your own. This seems self-explanatory, but most writers don't get the concept.

When you go into a book store, it shouldn't be the average buyer who was recommended something by his/her coworker or is just wanting to be "cool" by reading the latest *Harry Potter*-like series. When you go into bookstores like Barnes & Noble, it should NOT look something like this:

You walk up to the book-search bitch-guy/lady, you ask him/her, "Where is (*insert your favorite genre here*) section?"

"Sir/madam, it's over *there*. Anything specific?"

"No. Nothing specific. I'm just a reader who wants to explore but really I want to be a dick by buying only *popular* books because I'm that much of a prick and close-minded."

"Oh." Shrugs. "Well, the Starbucks counter is over there in case you want to *look* pretentious while being a total hipster!"

"Touché, madam/mister. Sound kick-ass." And you go off your marry way into the land of exploring pointless titles.

What it *should* look like is you constantly scanning, constantly soaking in any and all books you find. Give literally all of them a chance because, frankly, *you* are going to be one of them. This is the reality of you publishing your own work, traditionally or self-published. So show support not for the sake of supporting authors, but for the sake of learning something new that you didn't know before, or learning something about your tastes that you didn't know, either.

Look at copyright pages and know which publishers are which, look at the author's "also by," look at the recommendations in the back of the book. Constantly be reading and going from one book to the next. It should get to the point where you have such a long reading list that you don't even have time to be a writer. That's the kind of reader you need to be and the kind of reader you would want within your die-hard readership if you do publish a book. You don't want to associate with readers who buy crap because it's "trendy" or "cool," you want readers who actually are passionate about reading and know what is good and what is bad.

Once you are buying books like a total nerd, that's when you get *ta readin'* constantly! You have to be constantly reading and reading and exploring new crap. Always be open-minded, but always have a standard too. For example, when I pick up books, I read the first page. If it isn't in the style of the kind of books I like, I don't continue (sort of like how agents do). You pick up book after book and find that style of writing that you like — once you have read enough and found enough authors that fit the style of what you like — and then it becomes astronomically easier to tell the difference between what is going to be a book you are actually going to read all the way through, and what is going to be a book where after you read it you feel like a total dickhead for wasting your time giving it a chance in the first place simply because you were *told* it was "good."

Do not care so much about buying "best-sellers" or books on the *New York Times* list. That's meaningless. There's so many self-published authors that would blow James Patterson out the water (which by the way he hires ghost-writers to do most of his writing anyway) — so keep that in mind when looking at other authors' works. Always keep reading and always keep finding the specific kinds of books you connect with, fiction or non-fiction. If you like politics, read the heck out of politics; if you like mysteries specifically set in Florida or the Mid-West, that's what you have to hunt for. Hunting for the book is the hard part, enjoying it is the easy part. Always be looking for gold to read because if you find work that you love it makes you one step closer to finding the kind of work you want to do, and the kind of work that shows you what your book should look like (but obviously with your own personal spin on it, of course — don't be lame and copy writers like the *Twilight* Fan Fiction clown who made that "best-selling" *50 Shades* bullcrap).

Once you are actually a good reader who knows what is "good" or "bad," what you can get away with in writing, how stories work and are formed in a way that *you* personally like, and how they are executed, it becomes infinitely easier to write a book. Most of writer's block is because the writer has no idea what is good or bad or what their goal is in the project. That's honestly the key to writing something of quality is knowing and enjoying and appreciating things of quality. Also, if you pirate e-books, read them, and they are good, I would suggest then buying the e-book or something to support the author. Because the reality is that they need money to eat in order to actually be alive enough to make another good book for us readers. *Sigh*. And if they are already dead, eh, their heirs to the estate get the cash. Point is: support authors you like and that you deem worthy of support — but always be both open-minded and critical of what you are exploring. Always give it an honest shot, though.

1.2 Creating a goal in writing.

The biggest thing that separates successful writers from the crap ones is that typically successful writers have a clear understanding of their actual goal in doing a project. Even fiction-wise that is fully for entertainment purposes has a goal in mind. For example, as a writer you should always write exactly what is on your mind and what you are into in the present moment, regardless of it being marketable or sellable or not. Constantly be writing. Even fragmented crap like dialogue on a piece of napkin, or botched poetry on a cereal box's inner blank cardboard with a pen. Doesn't matter. Write exactly and fully what is going on presently in your life. Compulsively write and selfishly write whatever is on your mind or what is eating you inside. Because to be quite honest, that's really the only time you will ever come *close* to producing anything that can be "good."

Writing is entirely expression and should be treated as such. Even when reading you should know that what you are reading is a direct stream of the author's conscious existence and what they have deemed to be their "truth" or what *they* have eating inside *them*. You go into reading a book with that mindset, it then becomes easy to understand the work, its goal, why you are reading it, and if it achieved its intended goal. Once you have an idea of what the author's goal is in producing a body of work, and you read that body of work and conclude that the author did achieve their goal in what they were trying to say and executed it perfectly in their own specific way, that's when they are worthy of your money, support, and yes, recommendation.

It should be noted that Sally Fairfax, the name of the author of this book, is a pen-name. Reason being is because I'm not going to put my actual legit author name and be under the scrutiny of how "legit" I am or how "successful" my books are. The point is that this pen name is to show you that I could be a writer bum down the street from your house, or I could be James Patterson himself bashing himself to prove a point and is self-publishing this lame book just for shits and gigs. Is that the case? Does it matter? That's the point. I'm writing in this and my goal is to write it and tell you my advice on the matter. You buying or not has no bearing on me. I do not care what you think of my work, and you should be in that frame of mind as a writer, too; but also acknowledge and respect a writer when they do do dope shit in their work. That's why I advocate that being a "best-seller" is such a hoax in itself and does not showcase any absolute value in the work. Plenty of shitty best-selling books are out there that sell millions of copies still doesn't automatically mean they are "good." If your automatic goal is fame and fortune, you will have better luck just going to school to be a doctor or lawyer, because those jobs are much clearer in that goal set.

But, if you don't want to listen to that piece of advice from *me* — because fuck *me*, right?! — it should be noted that non-fiction comes vastly closer to making actual money than fiction does. That being said, when you write non-fiction it then becomes a matter of actually being an expert on whatever subject you are writing about. Literally anything can be non-fiction. If you are good at washing cars, write about it. Plenty of weirdos out there want to know how to properly wash their cars and they'll be happy to give you their cash in exchange for that info. If you are an older person who wants to teach young people a thing or two about common sense, write about it. Literally anything can be marketed and sold and published. When people are on the internet, sites like Barnes & Noble and Amazon are actually popular enough to have influence and guide a person to your niche book.

Lets say you are a doctor, though — and as it turns out, any medical book is almost always going to sell bigly — that expertise is valuable as holy hell and you need to fully take advantage of that education you have. But lets say you are not a doctor and are just a patient but still want a piece of the non-fiction medical pie in the book industry, then read everything on that specific subject you want to write about and just give your personal take on it. That's why copyright pages and disclaimers are important and will save your ass when it comes to buyers being pissed off that you didn't give them the type of "expertise" info (like from an actual professional doctor) that they expected. Even commentary is great for buyers. Literally the world of books is the freest piece of business you can go into because the content is so diverse. Anything can sell as long as it has some shred of value to it and is honest about what it's doing. Keep that in mind.

But if you are into fiction, you have to look at what kind of genre you are into. Read as many authors in that genre as possible, and then make up your mind if you want to pursue that genre yourself. If you are a person who enjoys reading about two lovers on a beach kissing or some crap, write romance that is specific to that setting; or if you like trolls, goblins, fantasy crap, and that peeks your interest, then pursue *that*; or, if you're like me, and gravitate towards cutthroat, gritty, provocative, offensive, taboo genres of books like Transgressive Fiction, then it becomes easier to find authors in that specific genre. Once you know your actual genre then marketing and actual *ways* of telling that story within that genre become so much easier and virtually puts an end to any writer's block.

A writer's goal should be exactly what they are wanting to say. As a writer, you have to simply say exactly what it is you want to say and do it unapologetically. Believe it or not, most writers who are successful have random-ass manuscripts of botched, pointless crap that they simply just purged from their brains, finish, and set aside with no intent on it being published. Or they just publish it under a pen-name somewhere, not market it, and just have it in print for themselves to give to random persons that give a shit about whatever subject it is. Most writers are creative, and if you are creative you're probably crazy, and if you're crazy you probably have issues that need to be resolved or talked about. Talk about them and put them down. Even shitty, undeveloped characters talk about crap they care about it and you got to imagine ways in which their conversations pan out. It's just writing. Just say it and get the first draft out!

1.3 Dis-importance of first drafts.

First drafts are always bad. Never, ever expect a first draft to have any actual coherent, thought-provoking content or have any remote level of quality. It's a first draft and should be treated as such. You should go into your writing with that in mind because it will save your ass. The first draft is purging the idea of what you care about down and out of your crazy noggin' — *editing* is what makes it quality.

Lets say in your first draft of a novel you have two characters talking about complete and total nonsense and the dialogue is so botched and unrealistic it's laughable: it doesn't F-ing *matter!* Put it down, out of your mind, and let that manuscript marinate. In fact, when you finish a first draft, just put it away and work on another project. Waiting on a story and having so-called "fresh eyes" is what makes the story actually well-rounded. If you see those two characters a month later and read them (especially after you have read or seen some movies or something in that month that enlightened you and gave you a "new perspective") and those two characters you wrote in that shitty first draft are actually on to something still, but still can be improved on, that, my child, is editing and polishing. But that first draft has to get down so it can actually be edited. That's the thing: first drafts just have to get down in front of you to connect the dots and make it better later. Once that's there, proceed with editing . . . and editing . . . and editing . . .

Keep in mind that stepping away from a manuscript and letting it take time for you to reflect on is equally just as important as the editing goes. For example, I was writing a novel that dealt with degenerate characters, but the problem was that I didn't have an actual scene in my head to go on. I had *ideas* for scenes — even some dialogue drawn out — but I had no experience and I needed that extra flavor and sight of real-life degenerates to actually make the story most realistic and believable, which was also part of my goal. Then a friend of mine invited me out to a bar. I went and it turns out my friend brought cocaine to this place. I didn't do the drugs, but I took it as an opportunity for my book and its research. I met my friend's dealer (a lovely man, actually,

16

though he was shirtless and in some random biker gang) and literally was so interested in his stories it was positively sickening to him. He probably thought I was a cop, and he asked too, upon which I showed him I wasn't wired or anything by feds. But even that entire process of proving to him that I was a "degenerate" (or "cool") like him and not a narc was part of that process and experience. He told me so many juicy stores. I even witnessed my buddy messin' with some chicks who were actual prostitutes. These are taboo subjects and taboo people, but god damn it helped me write a book that I am proud of and felt cool enough to actually publish and put my name on. It become a "best-seller." *yawn*

Always look at that first draft for what it is: purging. Just feel what you want to feel and say what you want to say and put it down. Do not give a single fuck what it looks like. Just keep reading, get influenced and inspired, and keep writing. Always keep writing. Always keep researching and living. That's another thing too: living and experiencing and listening to people and having an open mind is what makes a writer a "good" writer and how you can actually create a book that is worth a damn.

Write selfishly, research selflessly.

Remember that.

17

1.4 What is of value to you?

Majority of writers view recognition and fame as the currency of which you gain from writing. Obviously you should chase it, but don't go *expecting* people to *give* it to you. It's a byproduct of the craft and entirely secondary. Ask yourself these questions:

* *Why do I want to write?*

* *What, to me, is cool about writing?*

* *Do I consider myself to be utterly creative?*

* *What do I want to get out of writing and publishing books?*

* *What is a realistic goal I can set for myself that once I meet I can be proud of?*

* *What do I have of value to offer to a reader? And secondly, why should I even care if they value me to begin with?*

* *Whose opinion of my work matters? Me? A literary agent? A publisher? A reviewer? My mother, father, family, or friends?*

* *Who am I doing this for? Myself . . . or the world?*

Part 2: The Writing Process

2.1 The draining nonsense.

Now comes the bad part of writing: the *process*. For most writers it's the part that sucks the most because it requires gathering information on whatever subject or goal you want to pursue. Anything and everything is research and method-acting. All people can be potential subjects for novels (or even non-fiction). Literally everything is free-range and can add a drop into the bucket so-to-speak of book "goodness" or contribute to the book's "success."

The only way I can show this is by giving you examples from my personal experience. My second novel, which I will not give the name of, had to do with autism. Autism is still a fairly taboo subject for most of society, because we don't understand it fully and it holds a stigma. During the time even before the concept of this second novel came up, I was under lots of stress, depression, and "finding myself" (i.e. so-called "soul-searching"). It's lame, I know, but it is true. But anyways, I had to go to the doctor for my mental health issues. I ran into a doctor that suggested I get IQ testing done and a full-blown examination of my brain and cognitive anythings . . . Also it was covered under insurance, so why not, right?

I went. I got the testing done and what came back was a very vague answer that somewhat insinuated that I was autistic, more specifically Asperger's. Personally, while I do think Autism and Asperger's are a real thing that some people do suffer with, I thought they were totally full of crap when telling me *I* had it.

I called my mother and told her the diagnosis and it turns out back when I was 14 years old my mother took me for a same kind of mental examination as the one I just had done and they, too, the doctors, confirmed that I had Autism. This was a surprise to me that my father never told me, but she informed me that she actually did but during that time I was a rebellious teenager and wouldn't listen for jack spit about what she had to say, even though depression and mental health issues were even a problem back then. I did insane research on Autism. Not just for book research or anything but because I actually wanted to see if they were on to something. I also wanted to learn more about myself and who I was and where I stood as an individual to get specific, proper help with my issues I was dealing with. I stumbled upon the idea that people with Asperger's had issues with social skills. It fascinated me. And during that time I was dealing with women, namely beautiful women. So I merged the two concepts: beautiful women with Asperger's. *Alas!* a book idea was born.

24

Interviews, books, research, finding out issues of women within society, namely what attractive women go through when dealing with superficial men. I had a nephew, too, that was autistic, and he ended up helping me in the research and provided me with drawings to put within the book to make it appear more "authentic" to the story. During that time my biggest influence was J.D. Salinger's *The Catcher in The Rye*, so obviously Holden Caulfield, the main protagonist in *Catcher*, was a huge influence on the voice of my narrator I wanted to produce. I was also reading lots of epistolary-styled books like *Go Ask Alice*, *The Perks of Being a Wallflower*, and *The Basketball Diaries*. This, too, influenced me and made me want to explore the concept of diary-writing, a very popular genre in fiction that is by far played-out as heck.

But I didn't care. This is *my* book and I can do whatever I want with it, I thought. Nobody could touch me when I was writing that book. Not a soul. I even put purposeful misspellings, drawings, notes, footnotes, and handwritings within the prose to make it more "real." I did the exact opposite of what they tell you to do in college English classes. When I published that bad boy, it was a hit! Sold so many copies and still to this day I get emails from readers telling me how much they enjoyed it.

Honestly, the most gratifying thing I found that I personally enjoy is when I make a self help book and someone tells me that they enjoyed it and it really gave them some help and

25

peace on whatever subject it is. That thanks is enough for me to keep doing what I'm doing. That's ultimately what makes the tedious task of the writing process bearable is the idea of the potential reward, and, too, connecting with a reader. Reader connection is the ultimate privilege a writer can have: when you create something that perfectly articulates exactly how a person feels on a subject, there's no feeling or adjective to accurately describe the joy that comes from that. You have to have a taste of it to know what I'm talking about.

2.2 Sit down and shut up!

5% of writing is research, the other 95% is sitting down; and for some, add an additional 5% of drugs and alcohol and you're on your way! Kidding of course . . . *or am I?*

As much as I hate clichés, it really is helpful to have a designated space specifically for writing. An office, a park bench, a coffee stop, your favorite library. Any place you want that makes you actually able to sit down for a long time. That's all writing is is sitting down and having the object to transcend the words down in front of you. That's it. Writing is sitting. Nothing more. Sit there. As far as I'm concerned, if a beginning writer dedicated one hour a day to writing, and once they actually sit down to do it they freeze up and end up not writing a single word, I still praise them for sitting down that full hour and setting away that time for it. That's majority of why writers never get their book finished because they don't actually make time for it, clear their space, focus, and just simply *sit down!*

Consider three options for writing your story:

1. A Typewriter
2. A pen and pencil
3. A computer, or Smart Phone — *note: which I wrote this very book on!*

Typewriters are super cliché, but honestly after using one I can see how the feel of it actually gets the juices flowing and fully commits you to actually sitting down and making the words fall out. OCR programs on the computer can even take the scanned papers from the typewriter and put them into text format on your computer to give to editors, publishers, friends or family. But getting it out of you in whatever medium is the point of using that medium if it grants you complete comfort and freedom.

Some enjoy writing long-handed. Though I have to say I personally hate writing long-handed because of how slow I actually produce content. If writing it down with pen and paper is what centers you and makes you engrossed into the story you're telling — even just as a rough draft — then I condone it completely.

Computers and smart phones, though, to me, personally, are the fastest way possible to get a thought down, get stuff written, and get some dialogue out in the open. With the way technology is going, texting has become lightning fast. Hell, you don't even need to *type* anymore. Blind people can just dictate into a microphone on the computer or device and it simply places it into words. If even talking is the best way for you to vent out your words, by all means.

Hell, if you talk with anybody just have your phone recording and make that your dialogue in a book. Who cares? It's labelled as fiction anyway, and the chances of it even being read is slim to none regardless. Just do whatever means to make your writing most comfortable. My way is via smart phones — Apple iPhones, in the notes app. I just think it's perfect for getting my words out of me. Then I put it on the iCloud and into my word processor onto my computer when I edit. Editing is the part where I actually sit down. Writing the first draft I typically do in my bed laying down, while on the super bowl taking a dump at my day-job on break, or at a party my best friend invited me to that I do want to be apart of.

I write anywhere as long as I have my phone on me. That's my personal comfort.

To each their own, though.

2.3 Word structure.

Another important thing that you have to consider when diving into your manuscript is actually looking at how the book is laid out in front of the reader to tie-in with the actual plot.

For example, my first novel was blocked off, and at the end of every "block," or "chapter," I would either end abruptly or trail off (". . .") and the reason why is because the book was intended to be *a dream*. To actually make the book appear more like a dream, a dream doesn't have "chapter titles" before your opening sentence to that chapter. And dreams are scattered and often constantly changing. So basically the ending abruptly and trailing off mimics exactly how dreams act. You can do this in any way you want.

Consider Hubert Selby Jr.'s first novel *Last Exit to Brooklyn*. Absolutely beautiful. How he writes is extremely fragmented, stream-of-conciousness. He omits quotes and apostrophes. It makes the prose look cleaner, read faster and more rapid, and that's exactly how the story is too. At times when Hubert has to use an apostrophe for differences like "hell" and "he'll" to not confuse the reader, he will use a slash. So "hell" is turned to "he/ll" and so on . . . Very creative and a cool way to write. He went completely against everything English class tells you and he's a "best-seller."

That's kind of the point I want to make. If you write and somehow intend to write "The the the theeee theeee theeeeeee person went to *the* store . . ." then that's fine because if you can make the "the"s necessary, the reader will understand it. But ultimately you are God in your prose. You can do anything you want. But part of making brilliant prose is having a clever way to create the prose's style, like Hubert's, make sense for the story's sake. So keep that in mind too. Just have fun and experiment with it. Read a lot too.

2.4 Styling & Voice.

What's voice? you may ask. Writers always talk about developing their "voice." But what does that even mean? Well, in my eyes "voice" simply means what do you have to offer that other authors can't offer. It could be your content, it could be the world's atmosphere you create, it could be the way you speak words when you talk. Basically it means what sets you apart from other writers. Back to Hubert Selby Jr., for example, when I picked up his work and I saw how anti-apostrophe and anti-quotations he was, I thought that was brilliant because no author in the entire bookstore that I knew of was doing such a thing. Immediately I gave him a bigger shot, especially because his content often dealt with the gritty lifestyle of New York City, which I find fascinating. He writes in this weird mixture of third- and first-person. He narrates in third-person but when his characters talk he just keeps on going and doesn't have a paragraph break. So it will be like this: "Walter was going into the store and he was pissed as all hell. Waz tha big idea, punk? The Indian guy in the T-shirt behind the counter looks up from his new's paper, The fuck you want, Walt? Walt, he/ll just have to get over his hatred of the Indian guy." It's a botched example of mine, but you get the point. Also another example is Chuck Palahniuk's *Fight Club*. He does the opposite of Hubert Selby Jr. and *overuses* the hell out of chapter breaks by creating very poetry-like minimalist prose that is signature to Chuck's "style" or "voice." Everyone knows when you pick up a Chuck book you will run into this. My point is that finding a voice is simply experimenting with the prose as much as possible and finding something you think is cool or interesting. But again, none of it matters. Your novel is your novel. Though I will heed warning, when you do non-fiction it's probably better to not deviate from actual coherent sentence structure that way to not confuse the reader. But it's ultimately up to you. Your book, your rules. If the reader buys it, that's up to them to decide.

2.5 Subject matter.

Sometimes you have to realize that your subject matter also defines you as a writer. And by that I mean a reader, or even yourself looking at your own work, can view your very mind and personality in a particular view when looking at the subject matter you choose. If you often write of drugs, your readers are going to expect you have tried drugs, you know about drugs, or you have been into drugs at one point. But obviously if you write fantasy as your subject matter, though most concepts in fantasy cannot actually be feasible, the image of you outside of your book will be judged in that way, sometimes subconsciously. What I'm saying is that be mindful of image of your work/character studies. I write controversial topics. When my employer at some charity place discovered my books and saw what I write, it changed their entire outlook of me and they treated me way different. I got lucky, though. Some jobs will straight up fire you. That's why certain things like pen-names are needed to protect you from those kinds of things. But regardless, write whatever you want to write, just be mindful of the work involved and how it will influence you in your actual life, especially if you are a method-acting writer.

Part 3: Publishing & Marketing

Now comes the fun part of the book . . . And by "fun" I mean the only part worth a damn in buying this nonsense of mine, because it's dedicated to actually publishing your polished, finished nonsense and it making you money. (And possibly groupies if you're into that mess.) Though there is no guaranteed — mark my words. Just have fun, always keep pushing and trying. Failures are just as important as successes. Believe me.

3.1 The creative marketeer.

My all-time favorite living author will always be Chad Kultgen. His work is rebellious, funny, honest, very specific, and taboo, and I love it entirely. But what's even more interesting than just his writing is how he markets his books. I've actually talked with him personally about this. He has told me that the marketing sometimes, in his opinion, is also part of the creative process or part of his "goal" of the book.

Example: In mid-2015, Chad released a book entitled *Strange Animals*. It was a book about a college woman who was doing her desertion for a final to obtain her college degree. Simultaneously she found out she was pregnant. She decided to make a Go Fund Me page stating that if she doesn't get a donation of a couple million dollars (I forget the exact amount), she will abort the baby. But if she *does* get the millions of dollars by donations, she will keep the baby, put the money in a Trust for the baby, and that's that. The whole point was to see if Christian–Conservatives, who are pro-life and actually *care* about being pro-life, would put their money where their mouths are, from what I gathered from the book's goal.

Now, to get to my point, the book was to be release July 7th of 2015. A month before the date, an actual Go Fund Me page with the same premise of the book stated exactly what the main character stated. The Go Fund Me was to end on July 7th and nobody had a clue it was for a book promotion. It actually got quite a lot of scrutiny and buzz from pro-life reporters and bloggers alike, though in reality you couldn't actually donate to the Go Fund Me page. On that day of July 7th, 2015, when the Go Fund Me page ended, a picture of the book and it saying it was released popped up on the page. Loads of sales for Chad occurred, along with death threats, bad reviews, and a whole slew of other crappy things, like the publisher condemning his actions that they were not aware of.

That's brilliant marketing! The exact goal of the book was put into action, the release of it was advertised by an actual thought-provoking publicity stunt, and it garnered a buzz and therefore sales! That's a perfect example of how the actual marketing can be apart of the art itself of the book.

Chad's first novel, *The Average American Male*, had the same kind of concept as far as marketing goes, only the publisher was the one who did it. The book was exactly what the title was: a guy doing what guys do: thinking about women, sex, and dealing with a girlfriend and a side-chick. Brilliant book. Upon the book's release, nobody was buying it. So the publisher decided to front a couple thousand bucks to hire some actors and a camera crew to make three comedic short films all about a minute long showing actual examples of what goes through the minds of males during dates and awkward situations tied to thoughts of love, being suckered into marriage, and the like . . . They all went viral, and, in turn, sales of the book skyrocketed him to the "best-seller's" list.

All I'm saying in this is that marketing can be an art form too, and if you can make a marketing campaign that directly matches the concept of your book much in the same way Chad's did, you can get a buzz going. My second book I published was about a guy who was going to commit suicide in 24 hours. I had an idea to hire an actual news anchor on an actual local news station in my city that my mom personally knew, and I was going to film him at the exact building where my main character in the novel was going to jump off of. But I wanted the anchor to look convincing up until the end, when the anchor reveals that this was all actually a book promotion. Then the idea was to pay for

Facebook ads on the book to target watchers of that specific news station so they would recognize that anchor, click the video and get baited in, and then hopefully check out the book. The main goal in marketing is not simply to just make sales — that's secondary — the main goal is actually to get them just to *look* at the product you're selling for them to consider if it is worthy to buy. Not the same thing. You get the point. *Bleh!*

3.2 Your cover.

The cover is very important. If people are racist in real life and "judge a book by its cover," then surely when people are buying books in bookstores there is going to be a particular kind of reader that will love the cover or hate it. If an old lady who loves romance novels goes into a bookstore, obviously cover artwork depicting young lovers together by photograph, or even something more elegant like a photo of a bed sheet on a beach blowing in the wind or some crap, that will typically target that reader directly. When making a cover (if you care about making money), you have to think about your target audience and what they would probably like seeing when at a bookstore. If you know your audience is in their early-twenties and artists, for example, put artwork that you think would pop out at them online or in a bookstore. You have to think of the target reader and what they would love to see on a book cover. If you are having trouble, go to Goodreads and go to listopia and search keywords of books that are similar to yours and look at the general idea of covers. Publishers know their crap and know what sells. Get a rough idea, make it yourself in photoshop, or hire someone. Though don't plan on getting a return back on what you spend. Any money you put down plan for it to be gone for the greater good of making an awesome product.

3.3 Social media.

You can have at it with asking friends and family to click "share" on their social media sites, but nobody likes a please-share-my-first-book social media whore. It's best to get the word out ahead of time on the release date and then keep promoting the release date, even with Facebook ads. This way it'll be sporadic when the shares occur up until that release date. Then you make a page of some kind that potential buyers can check daily if interested. When people you know are fully aware of the release date and you simultaneously promote the day it comes, it's a lot easier for them to get excited about it. When the day of the release drops, have certain events going like book release events, signings, contests, giveaways, and maybe even promotional videos. Always take any blogger interviews you can. Always buy copies and always be handing them out in exchange for reviews. Reviews are critical especially if a buyer is on the fence about you and doesn't know if you are exactly worthy of them purchasing. Reviews by actual readers are what separate the big dogs from the little dogs. I don't care how prestigious you are or how little you are, if on a listing you have a huge number of reviews, that in itself is impressive because any author who is in this business knows getting *anyone* to write a review of your work is like pulling teeth. It helps to have an actual budget of how much you want to spend on these things and keeping to that budget. Always try to at least break even. If you want a return, especially on a first novel, know it's going to be a bumpy, tedious road because of your work being unknown. Always push and progress with every release you make.

3.4 Links, key words, and titling.

This should be self explanatory, but when writing non-fiction you really have to be mindful of your title, emphasis on the subtitle because that's where the key words are and it gives a very brief one sentence on what the non-fiction book does. Novels . . . *eh* . . . it kind of doesn't matter because in general nobody buys a novel randomly unless they are die-hard readers, and that takes skill in linking yourself and getting an audience to find your listing. It's a process of everything from word–of–mouth, easily linking the book to a blog, someone else, whatever it may be, and likability of the books, not to mention specific targeting of a particular audience. Basically though, don't count on fiction to sell well for you unless you have a readership already of people, or if you are popular in a field that you can advertise at and have people come out for support. Real sales typically come from book signings and actual author meet-up events. In person, and especially at an event where someone can bring a guest, it is astronomically easier to make a sale, both because of probably guilt and because nobody wants anyone to not succeed, especially when it comes to a tedious task like book-making or any artistic endeavor for that matter.

3.5 Persistance.

All and all, you really can't expect much out of the book business because this beast is competitive as hell. Everyone wants to get their name known. All you can do is try, be creative in your marketing efforts, and both know and target your specific audience you want reading your work and potentially liking. Once a book is out, though, you should always be promoting it.

Remember that you are a reader first, a writer second, and a marketeer third, and that goes for authors traditionally published too. They have to do the same thing you're doing. The only difference is the publisher gave them an advance, which by the way you unfortunately don't typically see any royalties from until the publisher makes that advance back. So often traditional authors are just promoting to somehow meet that mark so that way royalties can come in regularly without promoting too much after the initial book release.

Always be reading books and experimenting. Always have projects going. This is a business. The more books you have out, the better your appearance as an author is. Generally people will support you. But don't go into this automatically assuming you are worth something. Always look at other authors as better and always try to progress your work. Never give up when it comes to making quality content and always learn, learn, learn. Everything. Pick up all books and learn all the ins and outs of the books you want to make and how other successful authors do it and what works for them and possibly could work for you too.

And don't be hard on yourself. If you sell zero copies, so what! It doesn't always mean you *suck*, it means you need practice in a specific aspect of the whole book-making process. But yeah, I'm not gonna lie, if you do actually suck, keep writing but don't release something until you are confident enough in its value of literature. And if you need help, join writer groups in your area, meet other struggling writers, work together, build a community. Often they are the ones that can drift you in the right direction toward success. Or you can go the safe route and make a manuscript and work your ass off querying constantly-rejecting agents and attempting to be traditionally published. You can try, but never *expect* success. It's entirely subjective and everyone reaches success in their own way in any creative business. It's up to *you* to decide how you will get there yourself!

44

DISCLAIMER: YOU MAY OR MAY NOT ACTUALLY
MAKE MONEY OR HAVE SUCCESS FROM YOUR WRITING
ENDEAVORS BY FOLLOWING THE INFORMATION
CONTAINED IN THIS BOOK.

Congrats!

You are now on your way to being a crappy writer! Prepare to struggle for days on end and pulling your teeth out. But just know that you can actually be an overnight success in this business. Many instances of it happening to writers, but nobody exactly knows why anything goes viral. Keep producing work. Maybe you'll get lucky and run into a project that produces a huge buzz. Never hurts to try. Just always write and read and enjoy yourself and the process. Keep at it. Always keep trying and pushing forward. Even if you try your whole life, die, and posthumously you obtain success that you aren't conscious to know about, it was still worth it (in my eyes). This business shapes you and turns you humble. You will learn a lot of life lessons in it. That should be your ultimate goal: learning how to better yourself and your work. Hope I helped you in some way. I probably have a 1% chance that you actually feel like I didn't steal your money on this product. Oh well! Cry about it! *Bleh!*

About the Author

Sally Fairfax wishes to remain completely anonymous. Though she isn't opposed to wanting the world to know that she doesn't like Lions inside her Numbers.

Copyright

Did you enjoy this book?!

Please, if you would kindly go online to . . .

www.goodreads.com

www.amazon.com

Search the TITLE of this book and please take a second to post a review! Tell other readers what you thought of it!

www.ingramcontent.com/pod-product-compliance
Lightning Source LLC
Chambersburg PA
CBHW031332250726

48656CB00005B/2093